Trout's Lie

TROUT'S LIE

poems

Percival Everett

Red Hen Press | *Pasadena, CA*

Book design and layout by Alisa Trager
Cover image by Mary-Anne McNeney

Library of Congress Cataloging-in-Publication Data
Everett, Percival.
 [Poems. Selections]
 Trout's lie : poems / Percival Everett.—First editon.
     pages ; cm
 ISBN 978-1-59709-998-1 (pbk. : alk. paper)
 I. Title.
 PS3555.V34A6 2015
 811'.54—dc23

                        2015006425

The National Endowment for the Arts, the Los Angeles County Arts Commission, the Los Angeles Department of Cultural Affairs, the Dwight Stuart Youth Fund, the Pasadena Arts & Culture Commission and the City of Pasadena Cultural Affairs Division, Sony Pictures Entertainment, and the Ahmanson Foundation partially support Red Hen Press.

First Edition
Published by Red Hen Press
www.redhen.org

for Joseph

Contents

TROUT'S LIE

A Trout's Lie

Deep stream, swing,
nel mezzo del cammin di nostra vita,
undercut bank beside a gravel beach,
beneath the roots of willows,
slanted into some usual sense,
washed, turned back into eddies,
reflecting what the sun can't see.

Clouds twist into knots,
turned by coiled winds,
a distant push; a source?
where parts cleave and cleave
thick in the circle of the middle,
the whole of it, loose.

Then with a hand,
the full sun complete surface,
i sol tace,
streams along, lap-lapping
against itself, against its current,
against its own origin,
where dim hours wait.

The Second Quartet

I.

Let me tell you now,
This eve, this hour,
That I will not permit
A sequel.
Follow, follow me.
Words spoken to myself?
Aloud? When fire
Burns the rim,
The horizon that
Leans toward the edge
Of this flat world.
The gate will be
Made of bright colors.
Follow me through,
Or I will follow;
It doesn't matter.
Hans, lead the way,
The admission being
Anything but free.
X Marks the spot
While Darwin holds
The argument steady, silent,
Whispering into this
Colloidal suspension
That is now. Like
Boltzman without a Maxwell,
In some macrostate west
Of west, beyond the
Second law of disorder.

2.

The smoke, like all smoke,
Is strange, indoors, swirling,
Curling around the fans
That spin on the ceiling.
Clockwise, clockwise.
Will you hide behind the
Canvas curtain, stretch it
Beyond the stretcher bars,
Beyond Dedekind's cut.
With a cut will you
Carve a new path?
One that I will follow?
But which way?
Crossed and counter-crossed,
No length is all length is
No length at all.
It is you, you say, slash
It, slash it, slash it.
Make it new again.

3.

The forces, the forces;
I count them, fiercer than
Things, names, stasis.
Will the power will to power?
The end of that second
Piece for strings,
Cut at any point,
Stretching forever.
The end all atonal, all noise,
But no noise, the strange
Will not forgive
Arnold, ending it all
With an argument.

4.

The argument rings,
Bells on in chime,
No more right than
Pound and Eliot.
I know this as I carve
This casket of rubato
That there is nothing
More, nothing left of
Auden and Breton.

New Sadness

The patient tricks of time
are the edgeless edges of
sleep, asphodel meadows,
bricks falling to a sidewalk.

Terror, what is your shade?
Your privilege is to be none.
Will hearts eat brains?
There is a rhythm

somewhere, somewhere, tap
slap, mapping out a familiar code
no longer trusted,
a second circle?
Now all is simply spoken

and that is a pity.

Refraction

The question is, why is the sky blue?
I know the answer to this one, I do.
I say, it is because the sunlight
Is refracted through hydrogen molecules

                                                   :n the atmosphere.

He looks at me, tilts his head.
He knows that I am begging the question.
He is asking again, without speaking.
Is it blue? I ask. I hadn't noticed.
I have no idea why the sky is blue.

                                                   Do you?

He says, Because of owl wings.
That sounds right, I say, that sounds right.

First

I came to this sunny beach first,
walking far ahead of the others.
I regarded the sea and imagined
achieving a northerly under sail,

sailing toward that inner light,
that charges us from a distance,
like the horizon, but something else
altogether on this expanse.

I came to the edge of this sea
first, dragging provisions behind.
A chest filled with promises,
some dreams in a paper sack.

TASK

The dead are dead as dead and deader,
deader than wasps in the rain
and deader still,
deader than dead.
The dead are dead, let us put them
     into a hole, dead and deep,
     into a dead hole, the dead,
and cover them behind the gates of sleep.
Dead.
Dead.
Deader still.
Bury the dead, with green music,
and lies of reincarnation,
rough sheets and velveteen whispers.
Dead.
Dead.
Bury the dead and carve out that bit of red earth
from beneath our guilty nails with knives.

No Dreams

Do not sleep or dream:
Do not dream of hawk-like flight
Into some narrowed field of vision,
Of sliding down black-iced highways,
Pushing out against a long peninsula.
Do not dream of nursed gardens
Lined on either side by suffering,
Of Pantagruel made small,
Frost-surprised irises, or tulips,
Of a fine snow finding enough cold to stick.

At the end of the dream
Do not see, at the no-dream's close,
The flowers piled up like monarchs,
Like so many abandoned tires and
Car parts and schoolchildren, their
Singing faces like daffodils, like
Pansies in the back garden.

The no-dream dream that dreams
Of dreaming dreams dreams
To lie down undressed on a beach,
Without the no-dream dreamer,
The no-dream dream resting in the
Stalled shallows of an icy stream
With a mossy bank, a
Promise to join the current.

The no-dream turns itself,
Pivots, the dancer with only a leg left,
Retreating right into its own threat,
Converging with the dream that
The no-dream dream dreams to be.
The no-dream dreamer
That does not sleep, but sleeps
The no-sleep of dreams.

His Glasses

His face was never stone.
His eyes were ever fixed, but never hard.
The day he left he made a soft noise,
Almost no-noise noise.
He lay there like a drawing by Doré,
By no ways, no waves crashing.

No sigh, no whimper, no sign,
No sequence of blaming rattles.
He knew, knew it all,
Didn't care that he knew.
I sat with him that day while
Others readied, dressed, cried,
Practiced crying.

The box opened,
His glasses had been forgotten.
He might need them, who knows,
But I needed him to need them,
Wanted to see them against the faded wash
Of his skin; the yellow wash
Of years within.

Too much reality; it is
Always a puzzle, too close, too
Intimate. The doors swing open
For lilies and roses he cannot see,
Even with his glasses.

SELF-MURDER

It was so easy for us to be so cynical,
To laugh away the head in an oven,
To shrug off the ride to
Nowhere in a garage.
It was so easy to disregard
A certain kind of success,
To disregard the beauty
Of scorched-closed eyelids.

It was so safe from where we stood
To lock eyes with herbivores and doves,
Platypuses that eat who-knows-what.
So safe to follow, one finger tapping the air,
Counting the steps to the next bottom.

So wonderful were we, tap, tapping
The air in front of us, following our finger
To a better view, sitting on a bench
For a better, safer view,
As if in some dusty museum,
The floor, hard but willing to dip;
The ceiling, nothing but dull stars.

Winging the Beater

It's winging the beater
Every time, it is.
Light a shuck, my friend and go.

Don't dally by the fire's side,
Light the shuck and go.

Hold it high,
Find your way from blindness
Into the darkness.

Into night, take the shuck.
Come back and tell us what you saw.
Come back and tell us what you know.

Just light the shuck and go.

THE HALLWAY

You know that
the hallway is empty
but every time you
step into it,
it is not.

You know
the hallway is empty.
You will not
go there again.

Box

I do not want a box.
I do not want a grave.
Let me lie where I die.

Let me lie where I die,
All cozy and deathy.
Cover me where I fall.

Put some irises around me.
Something that does not dig deep.
I want the ground solid beneath me.
Which means you should move me outside
Just before the end;
No floors for me.
I will tell you when it's coming.
I'll make this gesture with my hand.
Look for that signal.
I might be too busy to talk.
So, put me outside on the ground.
I don't care whether a tree is near.
There can be grass or no grass,
Sand or clay or granite.
The moon will be out in the daytime when I go.
Look at it for me.
Utter some clichés.

SIBLING

Up one side
And down the other.
Wouldn't you hate
To be the brother?

The Hurricane

So much,
one might have thought,
Could be taken for granted.
But for the wake
of a tenacious dream,
In the runnel
of notions that speak of a thing in itself.
It all remains two miles tall
and twenty wide, malicious,
Velveteen, thick, barbed,
A wall of creature
at dusk, the nub
of the problem,
the wane
Of a moon that is not ours to see.
So much, so deep,
so fast, so long.
But for the wake of it all.

Point

A tired point,
but a necessary one,
is at the beginning;
the other
points queue up behind,
if there is to be a line,
if there is to be a plane,
facing infinity,
staring at infinite backs,
infinite faces,
infinite sides.
A tired point,
but a necessary one,
would tip, but lacks dimension,
always, still,
forever
mere location.

THE MIDDLE DISTANCE

The middle distance, he said.
A fancy way of saying we're not there yet.
Soon, but not yet.
Between us and the background,
Inserted there between my face
And the spidery horizon,
There, there in the *middle* distance.
Pee before you leave.
Bring some fruit, some water.
We won't need the map.
No map, no map, because
We'll never get fucking there.
Is the middle distance between
Here and there?
Or is it where we're going?
Aren't we there yet?
Give me an apple.
I've got to pee.

On the Walk down My Drive

On the way down dirt drive, I glanced left
At the horses nosing through the dregs of the timothy,
At the wooden white rail fence, just painted, finally,
At the trough that needed emptying, to be scoured.
A ground squirrel clung to the metal rim and drank,
Unconcerned with my presence on the other side.
The hot wire on the top rail had done its job;
The bay no longer chewed and bothered the wood.
It was a pastoral setting, one that I had worked
Hard to paint, to rebuild from a line shack to this.
But as I retrieved the mail, turned to start back,
My shoulders sagged, my fence was on my other side.
For the briefest second, the longest briefest second,
A flash, a tock with no tick, I contemplated
What throughout my life I had considered so often.
Like those times, I shook it off, denied myself.

Weeks later, while driving through the desert
Toward home, a mule in the trailer behind me,
I would consider pulling to the side of the highway,
Unpacking and saddling the mule and just riding
Off, like in so many of those films I never watched.
I would just ride into that expanse of sun and dust,
Worrying not even the sidewinder by my feet.

SURFACE

I.

it came of age one night,
as all things come of age at night,
the thought, the notion
that to make an image of the image
is to kill the image.
something, some thing, indeed,
for a time, a time like ours,
for a time like this one,
vowing as never vowed to never
let a picture be taken
of the picture that's been made.

2.

it may sound
like the notion
of those so-called
primitives,
people who tell time by
their stomachs,
by the moving
firmament.
it may sound
like a strain,
a chant about a bit
of soul-taking.
maybe it is more,
but more,
maybe it is true.

3.

record the song,
count all the notes,
copy the page, find
each word again,
in order, again.
now copy that kiss,
indicate where
the fire burned,
point to where
the tongues rested,
tell how they grazed,
pressed,
tasted.

4.

alive on surface,
with holes,
cracks where animals
breathe,
lurk, crawl,
eat, fuck, die,
but surface is never
more than mere
simple surface,
surface clear through
to the center,
beyond to where
the other side
is surface, too.

DISPOSITION

She never said
She could not care less.
She said that if
She was so disposed,
She could have
Cared less.

Shame

What do we
find here beneath
this avalanche of murders?
No after no, negation
after negation,
cancellation after . . .
another avalanche.
See there,
the tracks
of a whole human
being. Being?
The truth that
we never read, that
we so reluctantly
accept, is that there
are no new massacres,
no fresh travesties,
no original genocides.
We will not
cast our votes,
we will not
validate the lies
of this democracy,
will not pretend
that the radios,
televisions, screens
that they give us as
gifts in the darkness
will play any music,
yield any images,
tell any lies
but theirs.

These Are the Flowers

These are the flowers that
We have grown.
Pretty much what we expected.
Laid out so carefully,
Watered, pampered,
Maps of them drawn in notebooks.
Brilliant flowers, happy flowers;
The table always wears some
In a vase or can.
The roses fight off powdery mildew,
And so we do as well.
Rust, black spot, aphids.
The marigolds should keep
The gophers away, but no,
They are only redirected.
A rattle, wiggle, shudder of a stalk.
Down goes that daylily.

So easily they go down.
The gopher snakes do not seem
To dine on gophers,
But they are in the garden,
Sometimes looking like rattlers.
They sometimes are.

It is not the snakes that trouble me.
I do not bother over gophers.
The rust on the hybrid teas is forgotten.
It is the flowers we have grown.
These are the flowers we have grown.

How I Got Here

When I was but a boy
I would walk alone.
I often wore my gym shoes.
I got lost only once.
I never did find my way back.

MODES

As if a dream,
as if in a dream,
as in a dream,
You fold your arms against yourself;
Your eyes shut briefly, your face
Tightens against some coming thing.
       But the rest of you, gone,
falls from a nest of coins and papers.
Arms folded, as they are, self embrace,
Around the sweet, tender waist
       that is you.
If there were a god, it would lean
Against you, press into you,
Molest your brow with a
Searing, brilliant stroke,
remind itself of the nature of beauty,
of the rake of some wind across
water, an owl's music at dusk,
each sight, each sound, each strange
part of that foreign speech with
familiar consonants and not
so familiar vowels—pauses,

all in the Lydian mode, mind you—
probably in the key of F.

WE SHOULD

We could, I guess,
lie down side by
side and think.
Count waves, but there is no ocean;
count stars, but there are clouds.
We could find a deer trail to the water,
follow it,
leave sign for others and ourselves;
pick up litter
left by the indelicate.
We could say sweet things,
Maybe kiss. Or
we could recall the wind that
brought us here,
kiss as if for the first time
every time.

THESE BONES

You see
he has these bones,
here under his skin,
muscles, these bones
that he has never seen.
He has these bones,
he was told,
hard, now brittle,
curved, rounded, straight,
who knows what color,
or how his bones smell.
They connect
          to one another
by ligaments, attach
to him by tendons,
superstition, memory.
He hopes   his bones
will last the journey,
will not shatter
under pressure of time,
atmospheric conditions,
humidity,
bad decisions,
the day's politics.
His bones
are his bones;
they build,
like a game,
the posture
he calls myself.

BIRDS

happen upon birds,
hawks, owls,
far above our heads or
stone after stone
ledge up to some
medium height,
wrens, crows.

Then home to hear
the box, like
so much bad music,
chin-high like that,
like so much

        drama, breast-high
        like that, like

                so much yawning,

        crotch-high like
        that is the way
        of all men, isn't it?

piled on one another

              like stones.

JIM

All dressed in black,
he would climb down
from his perch on my
right shoulder,
squawking the way,
screaming at me
that I was not paying
enough attention to him,
his crowness.

He made that clicking sound
in the black back of his throat,
continued his march
to my open notebook
where he made a few changes.

On Fire

He believes that he was on fire.
He, at least, believes it now.
He does not know what he believed then,
Then in that orchard,
The butterflies, orange, pitch,
Hinged open like promises,
Covering the high hedge to the east,
The sun sinking and drowning.
Then, yes, on fire, just like
He believes now that he was on fire.

He really thinks he might have been.
At least he knows he believed it then.
Belief feels like that,
Felt like that, back in that orchard,
The plane's engine idling,
The butterflies drunk with the last sun,
With their own orange and black.
They were on fire against that green.
He had to be as well.

Such as It Is

When the plane shook
I understood a truth.
That death means little,
Scares me no longer,
But for the imagined discovery
Of little faces . . .
Oh, little faces, little faces . . .
Holy fuck.

Limits

In the darkness that is our room, I search.
Not for you, for you are sleeping, breathing that sleep breath,
Exhaling through that small aperture, good for playing the flute.
I search for a darkness within the darkness,

Where darkness is pure, Stygian, pure like babies crying
And the sound of the little frog in the garden that we never see.
My black darkness where I hide from work and find it.
My sweet velveteen, claustrophobic shadowy den.

In there is where I will find my sweet suicide,
The life-taking that leaves no one sad or grieving.
That self-infliction that takes so much from me, from them,
Yet leaves me fed in some perverse way.
Little bits of flesh carved from my arms, my neck.
Little bits of flesh that smell like me and are no longer mine.
Veins removed from end to end,
Laid out on paper to dry.

Why chop myself into tiny pieces?
Why record and replay those same howls
Again and again?

Why fuss with anything blank,
When so many surfaces are already full?

You are asleep. I will not wake you.
I will close my eyes now and find some other darkness.

I will close my eyes now.

Homeland Security

The big bugs crawl when the
                    lights go out.
Sing a song for freedom.
The dogged winged ones round corners.
Sing a song for the night.

Krittle, Krick, Krack, the legs go snap,
The buggies drag and yodel.
The limping ones stride away,
Dancing into the night.

The tavern's just a table leg.
The rings of Saturn call
For gazing eyes and wondering shouts
Of songs with no refrains.

But the big bugs pause in the light,
Scurry only after being seen.
Dance that dance, sing that song,
That song and dance for freedom.

The big bugs crawl when the lights die down.
The rest of us sit very still,
Counting blames and faults and sins
While whistling the tune that freed them.

MAYBE EVEN CLOUDS

1.

Count the marines
In the courtyard.
Their hair is longer
Than you expect.
They look like nice
Boys and bad boys,
From Vermont-and-Montana-
Following-orders-dumbshit-
Non-blinking-soon-
To-kill-soon-to-die boys,
Who might or might
Not, should or should
Not, but never would
Not and never can

                              not.

Not sure doesn't matter.
Doubt is a penniless
Customer, conscience
Waits for the weather
To change.

2.

And they sing,
Round and round and
Round we suspect, where
We'll stop everybody
Knows. In and out
Like an old man's teeth.
Up and down and
Round and through,
The clouds don't
Look like sheep.
Off and on like lovers'
Eyes, whistling.
Late and last and gone and
Lost, the bats in the belfry
Retreat. Slipping, sliding
Like a sick refrain,
Stalling, each of us,
At the wake.

3.

One says,
When I die, count
My fingers.
When I am dead,
Count my toes.
But do not

                              Count cadence.

Someone counted
For me when
I pressed into
This life.
It has been up to me
To count them
Since then.
When comes the time,

                              When I pause

To let the world
Bother around me,
Count whatever it
Makes sense

                              To count.

Maybe even each other.

AGAINST SENSE

I.

The line of time
Is past.
The line folds back,
Splits.
Two lines now, future, present.
The past
Is a circle of
Abstraction, regret.
Do not speak
To me
Of your remaining
Perpetual possibility.
None of this
Is redeemable.
None of this
Is ours.
Points point to,
Pinpoint loci
On a dimensionless plane.
But to what purpose?
To what purpose?
I do not know.
Ten years,
Secrets of this gunpowder
Plot are whispered
In the darkness
Of this ending.
Rehearsed lines
In the end are just that.

They come back,
They come back,
Worse, no better.
Were never better.
How are you, friend?
Never better.
Never better.
Always worse.
How does that
Wind blow?
Anyone will tell you
A foxhole
Is a waiting grave.
Warm? No.
Dim lights dimmer.
The line of time
Will not be
Interrupted, will not
Be turned
By noise.
Sing a wee song
Sing a tune that
Sings a wee
Song morning song
Play a song
That plays sing
That playful sing-song
Sing a tune
Play a tune
A song of awe
Of wonder sing

At night through
Sleep breathing
A song wee sung
Tune your song
Your tongue
To play notes
A sing-song sung.
Across the expanse,
Beneath the heat,
Far into the
Ragged fringe,
The wood, the glade.
Rage sing notes on
The outer markers
Range and count
Over the plain
Without a feature.
Where are the cactuses?
Who's counting now?
Against the droning
Voices in a huddle
We plot, worry,
Weave over what
Ship to scuttle.
A ghost ship
Grounded on a dry
Salt sea, the
Whole of it, a ship,
Smoke stacks
Smoking
Propellers propelling,

Survivors surviving.
That's a good one
We tell the purser.
He chooses a
Language, issues some
Rubbish and
We believe him.
But he will not
Believe you when
You say that all
You want is
To be loved.
Suspended here
Upon this wire
The words are song
As all conspire
To cling to
Temple prostitutes,
To put to them
A riddle.
Ask what eats
All day? What
Kills by night and
Lives right
In the middle?
Ponder how much
Your corpse
Will weigh on
Mars.
Remember what
The living do

On mornings
Just like this.
They change their
Clocks, wind up
Their guts,
Shuffle to the square,
Stare at one
Another, touch
Each other's hair.

2.

Now we go
Into the wild.
See a lion.
See a bear.
They see us
But could not give
A damn.
We admire
The lion's
Work-shy stride,
The bear's strength
As he wrecks
A tree.
Then there is a bird,
A hawk that flies
Up so high.
You admire her
Music, but
She could not give
A damn.
It might take
More time
Than you thought
To either disappear
Or die.
Read with me
While we wait.
By the river.
Regard your own

Reflection.
Leave mine to me,
Let me toss
Pebbles into my own.
Each one a sin
I have forgotten,
Plunk, plunk,
Plunk, plunk.
If I had a tail
I would wag it,
But not now,
For it wags me,
It wags you, too,
That gentle girl
In the library,
That mechanic
Holding a crush,
Even the bear
That has found
Berries, the hawk
That has found
A draft, the lion
That has found
Us.
Drop, drip, drop.
The vessel still
Fills.
A truth might
Find rhythm, though
Fall hard on the ears,
But a lie possesses

A familiar grammar,
Natural logic,
Murmured as if
Breathed into life,
A dream in stone,
Swan-white and
Pitch, pooled
In sweet warm
Embrace.
What does the grave
Share with you?
Sateless, wandering,
To the laughing pit,
Indolent, ice kiss of
The moon,
The moon,
Over which a bovine
Leaped, divine,
Distraction from
Language, acts,
The thought of
Pitiful Christ crucified, or
A pitiful thought of a
Crucified Christ,
A terrific mouthful
Of poison, an
Erotic book full
Of misspellings,
Turns of silence
Into nights.
What chance does

Chance have against
Thrown dice?
Insinuate me into time,
Entwined irony
Strangling the weary,
Aimless desire.
Where is my blind Giant?
It is all still life
In which there is
Life still. My life
Has eyes, dark,
Profound and immense,
Show a ruthless fury
Turned to rage.
Rage on, eyes, rage on,
In flames, on ice.
The night is not
Very far away.
The night is not
Covered with water.
The night does not
Inhale the stench
Of death that a
Still life must wear.

3.

Where goeth Goethe,
Speaking of Islam, are
We not all of Islam?
We have in short
No mercy, but
Spiritual paralysis.
Unfasten the gates;
The church is not a castle
The right hand
Dumb to the left.
Withdraw momentarily
From the action of
Voice.
And if, by some chance,
Your tongue becomes
Flame in-folded
Into a knot of fire,
Breathe my way
So that I feel the heat,
Inhale the stench.
Those ten years were
But a phase, a phase
That pushes on,
All made so simple
By the absence of
Objection.
We stand against sense,
Against far walls of
Sense, beneath

Great piles of sense,
Along massive rivers
Of sense, sense, sense.
Will you my honey be,
For you are a honey bee.
Be my honey, honey bee.
Imagined, so loved,
In a world of fancy,
Shuffling memories
And desires, solitude
And wet dreams,
The logic of sacrifice.
Yes, yes, you believe,
But do you,
Tell me, do you
Love believing?
When of a sudden
We hear the last song
Of those stubborn bells,
The ghostly wail
Of the inevitable
Inevitable,
When all shall see
Us stripped down
Naked to our skivvies,
To our bare asses,
When crossing the desert
Broken and unheard,
Will we love
Believing?
Believing this, believing

That, wondering
Just who killed the cat,
Sighing when the
Facts are sung
Realizing the truth
Is not for everyone.
But everyone's here
Except for those
Who are not.
Damn them to hell,
Give them shovels
And advice,
Let them have
Their paradise, and
Let them be
Oh so precise,
As they count
The steaming
Dead.

4.

Very well,
I heard it then,
A voice from Egypt,
A call from Naucratis,
And a honk from
His ibis as well.
Words presented,
Words jotted,
Words scratched,
Words croaked,
Words surrendered
To sense. To sense?
Chopping logos
For the fire,
For the father.
O Socrates, Socrates
We need these arguments.
All the while, we,
Each one of us, is a
Differentiated body
Proper, with a center
And all that entails,
Each piece of each word
Worsening the cadaverous
Rigidity of writing.
Our lies are stiff.
Our truths indebted
To the lies
For making sense,

Forming sense,
Lies teaching us
To see the truth;
Truth doing little to
Expose the skin or
bones of lies.
Not so much, not so much,
Is the call, bumping
Sidereally through
What we thought we knew.
We do not make
The horizon, but
The time it takes
To get there.
All the singing
Makes no sense.
Tie me to the mast,
Plug your ears.
Do not attend
To my pleading.
The music, the music,
Like the bite
Of a venomous snake,
The song penetrates.
Tie me to the mast,
Tie me tight,
Tie me fast
Until the sirens'
Song has passed.
There is no helpful
Remedy, no easy

Trick of the eye,
Wave of the hand,
Waves, waves, waves,
One upon the next.
Ocean, where lies
Your virtue?
Acting outside yourself,
Spring up from without.
Where is your virtue?
All this water,
Pushing against sense.
Water is, above all
Other things, necessary.
Water is above
All other things.
Where is this
Machinery of water?

Biographical Note

Percival Everett is Distinguished Professor of English at the University of Southern California and the author of nearly thirty books, including *Percival Everett by Virgil Russell*, *Assumption*, *Erasure*, *I am Not Sidney Poitier*, and *Glyph*. He is the recipient of the Academy Award from the American Academy of Arts and Letters, the Hurston/Wright Legacy Award, the Believer Book Award, the 2006 PEN USA Center Award for Fiction, and the 2015 Guggenheim fellowship for fiction. He has fly fished in the West for over thirty years. He lives in Los Angeles.